A Blessing in My Womb

Written by
Catrina R. Gaston

A Blessing in My Womb
Copyright © 2022 Catrina R. Gaston
All rights reserved. No part of this publication may be copied, photocopied, used, replicated, or transmitted in any form in any manner without the author's written permission.

For information contact:
Catrina Gaston at graychellt@gmail.com
Written by Catrina R. Gaston
ISBN: 979-8-218-010153-9 (paperback)

Professional cover design by Childbook's Illustrator
Formatting and book layout by Raja Haris Sulaiman
Illustrations by Childbook's Illustrator
Edited by Stacie Vitello Douglass

Printed in the United States of America
10 9 8 7 6 5 4 3 2 1
First Edition: September 2022

Acknowledgments

I would first like to thank God for the creative gifts that He has given me in Jesus' name. This book was written with the love and support of my sister, Shameka McDaniel. Thank you, sis, for all of your prayers, encouraging words of faith, and creative ideas. Thanks to my father, Johnny Ray Clemons, and my mother, Brenda Gaston, because without you there would be no me. I love you, thank you for all of your love and support. Thanks to my two brothers, Barrett Clemons and JaMarcus Gaston, for all of your love and support. Thanks to my three beautiful nieces: Karlosha McDaniel and Asia McDaniel for your love and support and, Indya Gaston for always lending your ear, listening to my creative thoughts and ideas, and giving me your honest opinion. To my brother-in-law, Carlos McDaniel, thank you for all of your creative ideas, input, and support. To the rest of my family and friends, thank you for your love and encouragement. I love you all.

Dedication

This book is dedicated to all the mothers who are carrying blessed nations in their wombs. It is also dedicated to the fathers--may God continue to bless and multiply your seed.

Preface

I was motivated to write A Blessing in My Womb after viewing a YouTube channel where pregnant mothers cursed their babies while carrying them in their wombs. Later their babies died, never making it into the world.

Proverbs 18:21 says,
"Death and life are in the power of the tongue,
And those who love it will eat its fruit."

Children are a blessing from the Most High God. We should speak God's Word over their lives every day. From embryos to adults, we must remember to pray God's Word, praise Him, and worship Him as the Most High God. We must also thank Him for our children, for they are a heritage from our Lord and Savior Jesus Christ and the seed of Abraham. Speak blessings over your children and speak life to them. The life that you speak is God's Word. Remember how Isaac blessed Jacob? Bless your children by speaking the Word of God over them and to them.

This Book Belongs To:

_____

_____

_____

_____

Chapter One: Introduction

Let me start by introducing myself I am _____ your father/mother. I enjoy spending time with God, family, and friends. I also like to travel. I met your father/mother, and I fell in love with him/her.

John 3:16
For God so loved the world that He gave His only begotten Son, that whoever believes in Him should not perish but have everlasting life.

I'm so glad God brought us together. I am also elated that God has chosen us to be your parents. You have no idea how long we've waited for this moment. Now that it's finally here, we can't stop smiling.

My smile is as wide as the Red Sea!
My heart is beating so fast, like the
sound of a bumblebee!
Oh, I can't explain this feeling that I feel,
but someday you will experience this feeling for yourself.

I couldn't stop crying tears of joy when the doctor said, "Congratulations, you're going to be parents!" Your father/mother and I were so happy. We couldn't wait to share the good news with the rest of our family.

I hope to be the best father/mother for which you could have ever hoped. I will love you, nurture you, and provide for you, but most of all, I will pray for you and with you. I will make sure I read God's Word to you every day. You are my heritage.

Psalm 127:3
"Behold, children are a heritage from the Lord,
The fruit of the womb is a reward."

Chapter Two: The Beginning

"In the beginning God created the heavens and the earth." Genesis 1:1. While creating the heavens and the earth, He created you and me. God knew that you would be my son or daughter forever in this life and for all eternity.

"Then God blessed them, and God said to them,
"Be fruitful and multiply; fill the earth and subdue it."
Genesis 1:28

God created you for a purpose, and I will make sure you fulfill that purpose. Jeremiah 1:5 says, "Before I formed you in the womb I knew you; Before you were born I sanctified you; I ordained you a prophet to the nations."

Jeremiah 29:11 says,
"For I know the thoughts that I think toward you,' says the Lord, 'thoughts of peace and not of evil, to give you a future and a hope."

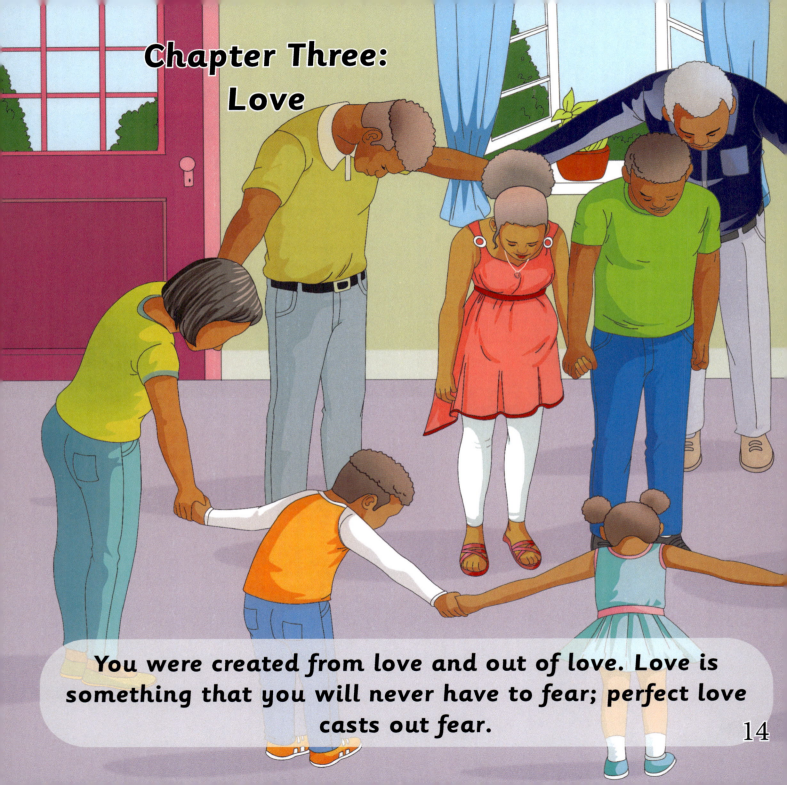

Chapter Three: Love

You were created from love and out of love. Love is something that you will never have to fear; perfect love casts out fear.

Your father/mother and I will always love you--your siblings and your grandparents will too. As a matter of fact, you have a whole lot of family who are waiting to love you.

And that's not all who love you. The one who created you loves you. God. He is love.

"For God so loved the world that He gave His only begotten Son, that whoever believes in Him should not perish but have everlasting life." John 3:16.

The disciple John says in 1 John 4:7, "Beloved, let us love one another, for love is of God; and everyone who loves is born of God and knows God." Jesus is love. "A new commandment I give to you, that you love one another; as I have loved you, that you also love one another." John 13:34. Love is something that God has given you for all eternity.

*I'm so excited that I can't sleep,
thinking about your tiny, little feet.
Your siblings are all happy and meek, waiting for that special little peek inside your baby crib
while you sleep so peacefully.
Your grandparents are excited too.
They've bought you a pair of little baby shoes.
Oh, they're so cute! I can't wait to put them on you.
I'm smiling right now.
Can you tell? It's like I'm living in a fairytale.
Oh, your heartbeat sounds so precious.
I can't wait to meet you.
Oh, how I'm so in love with you!
I just can't stop thinking about you and,
all the wonderful things that you and I are going to do.*

Chapter Four: The Helper

Everyone needs help when raising a child. We will have plenty of help when raising you. But first let me introduce you to the One who will stick closer than a brother will, the Holy Spirit. Jesus sent Him to earth to help you and me.

He will watch over you while you sleep and protect you from the hands of the enemy.

He will be your helper, teacher, and protector throughout your life. He will never leave your side. The Holy Spirit is the spirit of truth. We will always be sensitive to His voice and allow Him to guide us in raising you.

Chapter Five: A Reason to Live

**Psalm 118:17 says,
"I shall not die, but live,
And declare the works of the Lord."**

You should not die but live and declare the works of the Lord. You will live because Christ lives in me, and He lives in you. You will live and carry out the purpose and plan that God has created for you. You will live because that's what you were created to do. So live my child, for the purpose of God is in you.

We will forever seek the Lord on your behalf. We will always pray and ask God's guidance concerning you. God will lead, and we will follow. When I said that you were born with a purpose, you will live and fulfill that purpose. You should live. You will live my blessed and highly favored child. You are favored by God because you were chosen by Him. You will live for God. I speak life to you. I speak life over you.

LIVE.

Third John 1:2 says,
"Beloved, I pray that you may prosper in all things and be in health, just as your soul prospers."

You will be healthy and your soul will be prosperous. I will read a scripture to you every morning, noon, and night. Yeah, we talk to God over here. That's why we're so blessed and highly favored, and you are blessed and highly favored too!

God, I ask You to watch over my child in the womb. For he/she was created for Your glory. I ask that You cover them with the blood of Jesus. Amen.

Chapter Six: Image of God

"Then God said, "Let Us make man in Our image, according to Our likeness; let them have dominion over the fish of the sea, over the birds of the air, and over the cattle, over all the earth and over every creeping thing that creeps on the earth." Genesis 1:26. So God created man in His own image; in the image of God He created him; male and female He created them. Genesis: 1:27.

You were created in the image of God, so whether you are a boy or girl (that's up to Him to decide), all glory and praises to the Most High God!

On that day when you are born and placed into my loving arms, I'm going to sing praises to the King, giving Him glory for my king/queen.

Chapter Seven: Blessed

You are the seed of Abraham. Abraham obeyed God and because of Abraham's obedience, God blessed Abraham and his seed. Jesus is that Seed, and therefore, you are the seed of Abraham because of Jesus.

We are a family that laughs together. Sometimes we cry together, but we are still blessed. We are a family that prays together. We spend time together as a family.

I'll make sure I spend a lot of time with you. I will always give you a lot of hugs and kisses and my undivided attention.

Chapter Eight: Names

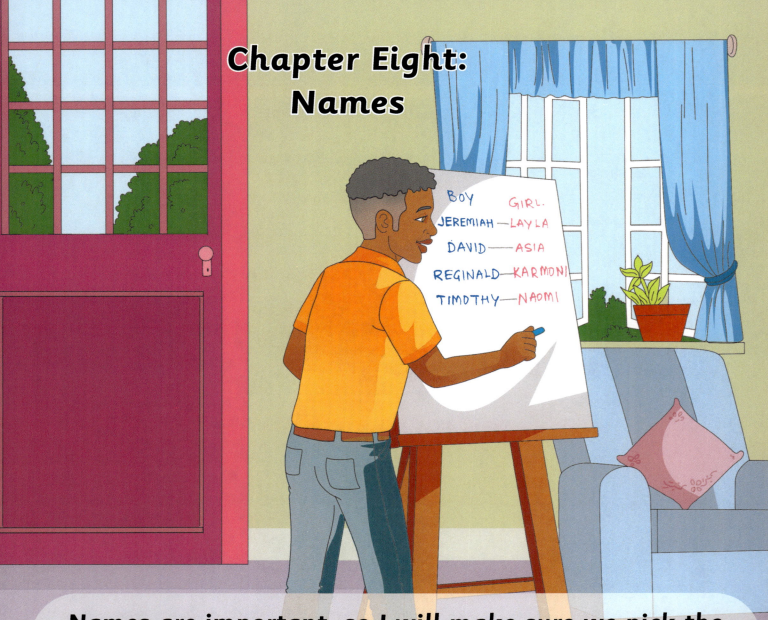

Names are important, so I will make sure we pick the perfect name just for you. (If you're a boy, we will name you _____, or if you're a girl, we will name you _____.)

We are still trying to decide but as of now, we will call you blessed because you are blessed and highly favored. Are you smiling? Yeah, me too. Oh, how I can't wait to meet you!

Your father/mother and I are wondering who you will resemble. Will it be me or someone in our family?

Well, until we meet, I'll keep reading A Blessing in My Womb because that is what you are to me. A Blessing! Someday you will read it to your family too. Daddy/Mommy loves you and we will always be praying for you.

Our Days of the Week

Sunday is our fun day. Fun day is our <u>praise</u> day. Actually, every day is our praise day, but on Sunday, we gather together with the saints in the house of the Lord to give Him thanks, praise, and glory.
Psalm 100:4

Monday is our busy day, but we will always make sure we take time to pray together as a family. I will pray for God's <u>protection</u> to cover you with the blood of Jesus, and He will protect you.
Psalm 91 and Isaiah 41:10

Tuesday is the beginning of the week, but still we will remain humble and meek, <u>planting</u> the Word of God and keeping His Word close in our hearts.
Psalm 1:3

Wednesday is <u>perseverance</u>. We will get through this week, praising and reading the Word of God to you.
Philippians 1:6

Thursday is our <u>patience</u> day, but we will still have time to play. We will have a lot of fun and play in the sun. I'll take you to the park or zoo, whichever one--it's up to you. Remember, I will always spend time with you.
James 1:4

Friday is our family time. Family time is our fun time. We will sing <u>psalms</u> while spending time together talking about our busy week, praying and asking God for direction for the following week. We will always remain humble and meek, so we can hear God's voice when He speaks. Remember when I said we can go to the park or zoo? Well, it's still up to you! I can also take you for a drive, while we both enjoy the sunrise.

Saturday is a relaxing day, but we still make time to pray, as we thank God for His <u>peace</u>, His mercy, His love, and His grace. We can also watch a movie or two, or we can go get ice cream--it's still up to you! I am happy as long as we are doing it with you. Cause spending time as a family is what we love to do.
Philippians 4:7 and John 14:27

TUESDAY

WEDNESDAY

THURSDAY

MONDAY

FRIDAY

SUNDAY

SATURDAY

33

About the Author

I'm originally from Mobile, Alabama, and I graduated from Cal State University with a bachelor's degree in television and film. I like to take long walks on the beach, go to Broadway plays, and dine in at some of the most exquisite restaurants in LA. I enjoy spending time with family and friends, as well as traveling. Family has always been important to me, and God has blessed me with an amazing family. I love my family, and they love me. I didn't say I had the perfect family. They're just the perfect family for me. And we believe in prayer. This is my first children's book. I felt the need to write this book to all the unborn children, using God's powerful Word, because children are a blessing from the Lord.

About the Illustrator

Illustrations by Childbook Illustrations
Childbook Illustrations is the most loved children's books illustrations and publishing agency. With 500 titles illustrated, designed and published, the agency is helping many authors fulfil their dream of getting self published with ease and affordable pricing.

www.childbookillustrations.com

ACCEPTING CHRIST

If you do not know the Lord Jesus as your Savior, I would like for you to take this special time to get to know Him personally. Ask the Lord to come into your heart and save you. Now is the time. Romans 10:9 says that if you confess with your mouth the Lord Jesus and believe in your heart that God has raised Him from the dead, you will be saved.

Romans 10:10 says,
"For with the heart one believes unto righteousness, and with the mouth confession is made unto salvation."

Lord Jesus, forgive me for I am a sinner. I repent of all of my sins. I ask You, Jesus, to come into my heart and save me. I believe You died on the cross for my sins, You rose again on the third day, and You are seated at the right hand of God. Jesus, I ask You to be my Lord and Savior. And I thank You for coming into my heart and being my Lord and Savior and forgiving me of all of my sins. I thank you for saving me. Jesus, You are Lord and Savior. Amen.

"The Lord is not slack concerning His promise, as some count slackness, but is long suffering toward us, not willing that any should perish but that all should come to repentance."

2 Peter 3:9

Please get a Bible if you do not have one. Read it daily. That is how you will build a relationship with God the Father and His Son Jesus Christ.

38

Made in the USA
Las Vegas, NV
23 January 2024